WALK WITH ME

GOD'S SOLUTIONS FOR

AMERICA'S HURTING CHILDREN

Samantha Allen & Sarah Webb

WALK WITH ME
Copyright © 2019 by Samantha Allen.

Printed in the United States of America

For information contact at
Samantha Allen - support@allenfamilyministries.org
https://allenfamilyministries.org/

Book and cover design by 4Tower.com
ISBN: [978-1-7338107-0-8]
eBook ISBN: [978-1-7338107-1-5]

First Edition: 2019

10 9 8 7 6 5 4 3 2 1

Jesus said, "Let the little children come to me, and do not hinder them, for the kingdom of God belongs to such as these."
—Matthew 19:14

They say ships are safe in harbor,

But that's not what they're for.

Yet steel-cut spines and iron sides

Now rest on ocean floor.

The risk is in the voyage

And the courage, in the task.

Storms may come with salty fray—

true men do not turn back.

They set their sights on Zion

And prepare for costly war;

To accomplish any greatness

Is to befriend great loss before.

Nations hanging in the balance

Are crying out for men like these,

To take the sword that is the Word

And pray on bended knee.

To go, to run, to sail beyond

The comfort of this land;

America, you're meant for more,

Volunteer and raise your hand.

Remember the roots that raised you

And re-find the Ancient Book.

Listen close for the call

As it echoes to all:

Who will go?

Who will willingly be spent?

— "Go" by Nicole Forber

CONTENTS

INTRODUCTION

Build up, build up, prepare the road!

Remove the obstacles out of the way of my people.
—Isaiah 57:14

AT THE AGE OF SIXTEEN, I became a foster mother to a toddler named Jason. Jason's mother was living at a homeless shelter that my youth group volunteered for in inner city Houston, Texas. With eight children, including Jason, his mother was too ill and burdened to be able to properly care for him. As we were volunteering at the shelter each week, my heart became moved with compassion for

Jason, and I knew I had to do something, anything, to help. I knew that even as a high school teenager I could make a difference in Jason's life and be a help to his mother in some way. That heart tug eventually led to the idea of becoming a temporary foster mom. My parents and youth group leader did not want to dampen my enthusiasm for caring for the poor, so my mother agreed to care for little Jason while I was attending school and hostessing at a local restaurant after school. Their support provided me with opportunity, wisdom, and guidance on my journey toward learning to care for these little ones growing up in immense brokenness.

As long as I can remember, there has been a special place in my heart for children—especially abandoned, neglected, and disabled ones. Don't be discouraged if you don't think you have the same heart for children. My hope for this book is that it will provoke you toward taking the first step in caring for God's children by being consistent in prayer. A simple prayer of obedience for a tender heart can have an enormous impact for generations to come. God says this about Abraham: "Through your descendants all the nations of the earth will be blessed—all because you have obeyed me" (Genesis 22:18, NLT). When we take a step of faith in obedience, no matter how small, blessing awaits.

One day recently as I was swimming laps at my fitness club, I pondered on the chapter titles of this book and the time it would take to write it. The Holy Spirit gently spoke to me and said, "This is their book." And I agreed. They are the innocent unable to speak for themselves. They are why we write. This book is for them. I believe the Lord told us to prepare the way for them when He prophesied, "Build up, build up, prepare the road! Remove the obstacles out of the way of my people" (Isaiah 57:14).

With this being said, let us prepare the way for His children to come to Him. Let us partner with Him to remove the obstacles in their way. May our words and prayers here help cut a path through their lonely woods, set up stepping stones in the mire they find themselves in, and shine light into their darkness. May we grab hold of their hands and walk with them, that they might easily find the arms of Jesus.

Despite what we may hear in the news, I believe abortion is nearing its end in our nation, and the question is already resounding in the empty abortion clinics and in our churches: Who wants the children?

PART ONE: STORY

Samantha and Steve Allen

Little Me

Two roads diverged in a yellow wood,
And sorry I could not travel both
And be one traveler, long I stood
And looked down one as far as I could
To where it bent in the undergrowth;

Then took the other, as just as fair,
And having perhaps the better claim,
Because it was grassy and wanted wear;
Though as for that, the passing there
Had worn them really about the same,

And both that morning equally lay

In leaves no step had trodden black.

Oh, I kept the first for another day!

Yet knowing how way leads on to way,

I doubted if I should ever come back.

I shall be telling this with a sigh

Somewhere ages and ages hence:

Two roads diverged in a wood, and I—

I took the one less traveled by,

And that has made all the difference.

— *"The Road Not Taken" by Robert Frost*

MY FORMATIVE AND CHILDHOOD YEARS were spent in a little village in New York called Lewiston. Lewiston was your typical small town of a couple thousand people, which I now think of as my shire. We had peach festivals in the summer and leaf jumping in the fall. I remember eating fried clams served up in take-out boxes in the square beside the baseball diamond on hot summer nights when my mother didn't want to cook. As we waited for our order number to come up, my brother and I pumped our tartar sauce into little paper cups and decided what flavor custard we were having afterward. Not that there were a lot of choices. It was either chocolate or vanilla. Cool weather brought the thrill of collecting apple drops and pressing our own cider. We would set it out on the back porch to let it ferment just enough for that tangy zing. Winters were magical on Main Street when Christmas came. Shops opened their doors and served hot cider and cookies to rosy-cheeked, snow-covered shoppers. Looking back now, I realize just how much of a fairy tale it was in Lewiston, New York.

I was convinced my house was the best house on the street because of our double lot and great climbing trees. My dad made us a swing on the big scotch pine tree in the front yard where I would gather my friends and climb so high we could see my best friend's house all the way at the other end of the block. We spent long summer days catching salamanders under the rocks on the hill and building forts. The creek behind my house would freeze over in the winter season and create an ice-skating experience that felt like a winter wonderland. Just the simple act of going outside to play filled me with awe and wonder.

My Good Father

One fall, my father and grandfather decided to build an addition onto our little 1941 house. I got to be the gofer, fetching nails, hammers, shingles, and even climbing onto the roof once it was in place. I was my daddy's little girl and his best helper. It seemed as though he could do anything and fix everything. He has eyes the color of the summer sky and a jaw that delivers his top teeth under, rather than over the bottom ones, but it's all charm to me. He has the mind of an engineer, always thinking of a clever way to do something better. His anger can flare in a moment, but it's never been directed toward me. His heart is as soft as that custard on Main Street, especially toward children. Dad has always been strong and seemed to make everything right. I'll always remember the notecard he had written in his engineer script and posted beside his office phone: Family First. And he did put us first. He was my protector, and I always felt safe with him. My parents weren't perfect but they loved each other, and we had a good family. At that time, I had no idea how rare my family and childhood actually were in this little Shire bubble.

My good daddy made it easy for me to connect with my good heavenly Father. I wanted to give Him my heart without reservation, so at nine years old, I dedicated my life to Jesus. I never doubted His existence because I could feel Him in the breeze, feel His power in the pounding falls of the Niagara, and truly see Him all around me in creation. On September 5, 1978, I was baptized and entered into the fold of those ninety-nine found sheep Jesus talked about (Matthew 18).

God's Heart for His Children

For forty joyful years, I've walked with the Lord. In this time of fellowship with Him, my understanding of His heart for children has constantly grown. Visits to inner cities like Houston opened my eyes to the reality that my childhood was not a representation of the experiences the majority of the world had. In my travels throughout many different nations I've repeatedly seen the brokenness in orphanages. I've allowed God to stretch my heart of flesh to feel the pain of those orphans as well as many other children. In doing so, I've been able to receive more of His Father-longing compassion for His children.

I grew up in a faith that takes God's Word seriously. When I read it, I am compelled to ask myself, What does this passage mean? Why did He choose this verse, this passage, to remain in the living book of His heart? What does this mean for me, my family, my nation, and the world? His Word is my Holy Mirror, and as I gaze into it, I must go away changed.

So when God says that children are a gift and a reward (Psalm 127:3, NLT), I have to ask myself and my culture some questions: Do I want a gift? How many? Similar to the gift of speaking in tongues, I may not understand everything about the gifts. However, I can choose to receive them in faith from the Good Giver and trust His goodness. His ways are not our ways, and it would be foolishness not to trust Him. That would actually be unbelief. If we know what our Father values—in this case children—why don't we as a church value them as we should, as He does? Why is it so difficult to get volunteers to teach children's Bible classes or hold babies in the nursery?

Jesus taught, "Let the little children come to me, and do not hinder them, for the kingdom of heaven belongs to such as these" (Matthew 19:14). When I look at the overwhelming number of orphans in the world or the 440,000 children in foster care in our country alone, I can see exactly what hinders their coming to Jesus. Since love nurtured in a family first reveals God and His love to a child, those who are abused and neglected receive an opposite view of our heavenly Father and His love for us. From the Holy Trinity to Adam and Eve and now today, God shows us His care and salvation through the context of family and relationship. However, for many children, lies about who they are and who God is begin when they are little and they have no one to show them the way. By the time they reach their teenage years, those lies often so harden their hearts that God's love falls on their hearts like rain on a tin roof, every drop running off unreceived.

King Jesus waits with open arms to receive all His children. He longs to give them His kingdom, but they hold back, shackled to false images of Him. Without loving families, these children remain adrift on a sea of loneliness. With no one to take their hands and lead them to Jesus and pray for them, their obstacles are almost insurmountable. Only the strong can make their way past the hindrances that come with being an orphan. Jesus has left the ninety-nine to retrieve the weak one who is alone, lost, and vulnerable. Reread Matthew 18:2, where Jesus calls a child to come and stand with Him to try to teach His disciples how to have faith. I think that child might still have been standing there with Him in verse 12 when Jesus told the parable of the lost sheep. Maybe that child crawled upon His lap. Maybe our Jesus stroked his hair. If I know Jesus, I'm sure He looked into that child's eyes with deep wells of love to let him know he was going to be okay. That He loved him deeply. And then, as He held on tightly to this little defenseless sheep, Jesus spoke these words straight from Abba's heart to those that would follow Him, "Your Father in heaven is not willing that any of these little ones should perish" (verse 18). Will we also take the hand of Jesus as He goes with us to retrieve His lost little ones and lead them home?

We Cannot Be Silent

How can we remove those chains that restrain them from the same love we feel? If love covers a multitude of sins, how can our love bring them closer to Him who is Love? We must ask ourselves these questions and truly seek out His counsel on how to bring Him the reward of His suffering.

Just like those that stood by and observed the victims of the Holocaust going to their destruction, we are also eyewitnesses to this heartbreak in our nation. We must not be silent. There will be an accounting. We must open our eyes, our ears, our arms, and our homes to their pain. We must begin to dialogue with Jesus for His plan in redeeming these little ones.

If you recall, in the Genesis story of Cain and Abel, Cain killed his innocent brother, Abel, out of jealousy. Father God heard from heaven and was so displeased as Abel's innocent blood cried out from the ground (Genesis 4:10). Still today, innocent blood cries out to its Maker, and God's love is jealous to defend His little children. Not only will we have a personal accounting on Judgment Day, but God will call the nations to account. He will not forget the blood of the aborted, trafficked, and abandoned in America because He is a good, good Father. He has written each one on the palm of His hand. It's time for us to open our clenched fists and write the name of the lonely child there. We must then grasp the child's hand and walk with him or her to the Good Shepherd.

The Closet

The greatest thing anyone can do for God and man is pray. It is not the only thing, but it is the chief thing.

—S. D. Gordon

S OME BOOKS ARE BEST READ in your prayer closet. Not in your comfy armchair by the crackling fire, but on the hard floor of your closet with your heart fully engaged, asking the Holy Spirit for an impartation of the Spirit of wisdom and revelation. I would encourage you to read this book in that place of prayer. Ask Him to speak to you, to help you shake off fear, ungodly beliefs, and apathy.

Then ask God to reveal His sweet kernels of truth to you. Lay down your misconceptions about His children as you lie on your face before Him. He will be faithful to illuminate His Word to you and share His heart with you. When you ask, He will uncover the unimaginable gifts and surprises He has waiting for you, tucked away in the hearts and hands of His children. However, you will only find these gifts when you venture by faith into that place in His heart.

So many resources are available now to aid adoptive and foster families, including grants, books, and support groups. Adoptive and foster care agencies are now meeting the great need to provide continual support to families after children are placed with them. Friends and church family increase in importance as they step in to offer support. And yet, just like a kitten digs in its claws to hang on when it's afraid, we, too, must cling to our prayer closets in our journey with hurting children.

The walks we take with these children are hand-holding, chin-lifting, alongside-embracing, walking-in-their-shoes-for-a-piece journeys. We just love them to the best of our abilities and lead them to Jesus, where He does all the heavy lifting of burdens, saving, and washing. He is the only "Great Fixer-Upper." As we walk the path together we learn of His names as Healer, Redeemer, Hope, and Ashes to "Beauty-er." We get to pray our hearts, guts, and brains out, but He is the only one who can give them what they need.

We can never overestimate the power of prayer and fasting to heal these children. Chances are, these children will come out of brokenness with love banks that might only have a couple of dollars placed in them by a broken parent, relative, coach, or teacher. But if we peer into their prayer buckets, clanging behind them as they go, they are usually dry as a bone with prayerlessness.

In March 2019, a deadly EF-4 tornado ripped through Alabama and Georgia, killing twenty-three people. One Alabama family took refuge in their grandmother's prayer closet, and they were all saved while the rest of the house was destroyed.

Prayers for Jezreel

Before she was ever born, our prayer life for our adopted daughter, Jezreel, had already been an adventure. Since my husband, Steve, and I knew before we were married that we wanted to adopt a child, the Lord would bring her to mind in prayer throughout our years of raising our own biological children. While serving as missionaries in Bangkok, Thailand, we felt that the Lord had released us to fully pursue adoption. Jo, a friend of mine halfway across the world in Dallas, Texas, began to join us in prayer for a little girl in China.

I'll share more about the amazing journey we had in finding Jezzie later. However, in this chapter on prayer, I want to share some of our adventures that forced us out of our prayer closet to pray in some pretty amazing places and situations. Soon after Jezreel arrived "home" to our home in Bangkok, we had to take her to the United States to obtain her citizenship as an American. She also had to have a much-needed heart surgery in the States. Jezreel has only one ventricle in her heart and had been blue since birth due to lack of adequate oxygen. Upon discovering this, I was so glad we had already been praying for her since before she was born! Most babies with a condition as serious as hers were left in the dying room of the orphanage. In the United States, children with congenital conditions such as hers receive the appropriate surgery soon after birth. Jezreel would be four years old when she finally was able to receive her new lease on life.

No insurance would cover her, since her condition was congenital, so before we returned to the States from Thailand, we worked with our contacts there to find someone who would perform her surgery pro bono. We searched for a compassionate, gifted surgeon and hospital that would commit to doing her operation for free in Dallas, Texas. We thought our contacts had been able to secure the surgery, but the week before we were scheduled to fly home, it all fell through. Our time in America was limited since, as missionaries in Thailand with an engaging and growing church plant, we felt we couldn't be absent for more than a couple months. So, we kept on praying.

Answered Prayers

My father worked as an engineer in hospital construction at the time in Dallas, Texas. He had heard of a newly arrived pediatric heart surgeon with a stellar reputation at Medical City in Dallas. Somehow, this new grandpa got the surgeon's phone number and called him, left a message about his new granddaughter, Jezreel, and asked him to do the surgery. Not only did the surgeon return the call while he was driving home in his fancy sports car, he said yes to my father without ever even meeting with any of us!

Our next hurdle was to get the hospital and the rest of the medical team to sign off on this complicated surgery called a Fontan procedure. This surgery would rework her artery "plumbing" and get her the oxygen she desperately needed. Weeks of waiting stretched into months, and it was hard to remain steadfast in prayer. My family drove to 7777 Forest Lane in Dallas and Jericho-walked around Medical City seven times. Our whole entourage of seven may have looked a little silly making our laps, but we didn't care.

And then we waited.

As I agonized in the waiting, Steve was full of peace, saying that the Lord was taking the time to heal her heart, before He healed her physical heart.

Then one day the call finally came. Medical City agreed to cover 80 percent of Jezreel's surgery, and the entire surgical team signed off to do it pro bono! Her surgery was scheduled for Valentine's Day 2006.

We started the day of the operation early and with so much excitement. With the perfect Valentine story in the making, a news team arrived at the hospital to cover this little Valentine girl basically getting a new heart. The local radio station got wind of her story, too, and covered it as well. As we waited, visitors came and went, but what was supposed to be a three- to four-hour surgery turned into thirteen hours. This amazing surgeon that God chose, delicately cut through layer after layer of scar tissue. Finally, close to midnight, they completed the surgery and let us see her briefly.

The surgeon tried to prepare us for what had happened and what to expect when we first saw her, but the sight of her there, hardly

recognizable and hovering between life and death, sent her daddy back
out of the room weeping. Jezreel's face was puffed up like a balloon,
and her chest had been left open to accommodate the swelling. A thin
layer of Gore-Tex, like a window into her chest where so much had
just transpired, revealed her big amazing heart beating away. The web
of tubes threading in and out of her body and the numerous monitors
filling her room made my legs go weak and my breath escape. It was a
moment I will never forget.

Afterward, we went into the waiting area where we collapsed onto
stiff couches. There we phoned all our prayer warriors to ask them to
intercede for her as she fought for her life once again. In the blur of
the ensuing days, her lungs, kidneys, and liver all failed after such a
prolonged time on the heart and lung machine. Day after day, all her
prayer warriors kept the pediatric intensive care unit—the PICU, as
it's called—busy as they took turns going back to her bed to pray for
her. It was an exhausting time as we also had sick children at home
experiencing an American strain of the flu for the first time. Fevers
didn't just last for days but weeks, and it felt as if we would never see
the sun.

From Death to Life

One day, I stole away to a coffee shop across the hospital to meet
with a friend. I was hoping to enlist her sympathy, but instead she told
me was how lucky I was. She looked straight into my bleary eyes and
told me what an honor it was for me to witness such a beautiful soul
take flight and refuse to die. What a gift it was to watch and pray in
breathtaking wonder and walk this child from death to life, and to be
the mother of such a person. I sat there quiet, soaking in that truth
for a long time.

On the day of that surgery, Jezzie and our whole family put on
our spiritual running shoes to run a marathon that would consume

all our strength and resources. The cost of her surgery and hospital stay escalated to a million dollars by the time it was all said and done. Needless to say, we did not have that 20 percent of the hospital portion that amounted to $20,000. Walking the cul-de-sac one morning in front of Steve's parents' condo, I prayed and looked upon the vast amount of money still required to pay that bill. Now that she was finally on the mend, we felt desperate to get back to our mission field in Bangkok. The Lord clearly spoke Psalm 37:25 to me and reminded me of David's prayer: "I was young and now I am old, yet I have never seen the righteous forsaken or their children begging bread." God showed us his great faithfulness through the generosity of friends and churches and family, and we owed not one penny by the time we returned to Thailand.

The Prayer Bucket

In addition to loving these precious abandoned children, we must fill their empty prayer buckets for the fights they have ahead of them. All our online research, doctors, specialists, therapists, books, and seminars will never substitute or be enough for their need of the heavenly Father. The Maker of heaven and earth created these children and knows every single thing about them, every single detail of their lives. He loves them more than we ever could. Jezreel got to meet Jesus through the faith of our family, thankfully, but He has known her intimately since she was in her mother's womb. He has her plan, her Book. I must believe that even though her birth parents abandoned her for reasons I cannot begin to comprehend, He never once has forsaken her.

Some amazing God-breathed therapies are available out there. But I know the best, most important thing I can do for Jezreel is to fill her prayer bucket to sloshing, overflowing. Then I will have done my very best. Then I will have fought her battles and demons with the true spiritual authority of a parent. That is a mighty, mighty thing. Whatever else we encounter on this perilous expedition with Jezreel, I know we will have won if her love bank is full and her prayer bucket overflowing. It is then that the heavenly Advocate is released to do what only He can do.

The prayer closet is a place for us to faithfully enter into. We are the weak vessels. This task of unconditional love is not for the faint of heart. Daily time in my closet is required for a fresh infilling to go the distance. It's only there that our tears and prayers will actually move heaven and earth for our children. If you are contemplating on how to love His children, in any shape or form, you must start in the closet and finish in the closet. I never want to be guilty of giving Jezzie clean pajamas, a full tummy, and toys without end, until I have filled her prayer bucket with the power of heaven on her behalf.

Jezreel: God Plants

Little Girl wobbling
Her name was sick and weak.
Crying, fainting, pining hard
Steel all cold, but eyes with spark.

Life O Life
You cannot be destroyed!
When Author writes it,
Nothing will be dismissed.

Looming dams in every freedom river
Sharp sticks that jab and poke

Nothing seen, only dreams
But we know that child Hope.

Hear the sound of branches breaking
Cracking as they loose.
Life is a torrent and is not
Held at bay.

Digging, scratching shallow roots
Barely hardly in frozen sand
Up up in Gentle Hand
To carry over ocean and land.

Into fertile ground
Sun warming earth fragrant.
Flowers, green, roots deep for water
Umbrella of love protects.

Tender shoot beginning
Water and sun water and sun
Water and sun
Water and sun.

Now look at this sapling!
Every green leaf shouts, "The Gardener!"
I see her Deliverer, Transplanter
Rejoice at the work of His hands!

—"God Plants" by Samantha Allen

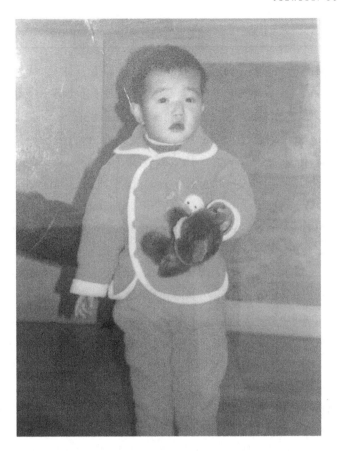

Jezreel Allen, age two

GOD IS THE PERFECT GARDENER. Everything good in this life begins as a seed, according to His design. The redolent smell of the prepared soil, the illumination and warmth of the sun, and the epic quest of the tiny hard seed have always thrilled me. Since I was a little girl, the garden has been a favorite spot of mine. As a wife and mother, springtime and the promise of the seed beckons me from the complexities and responsibilities of my family. Ultimately, the joy my garden brings me is that, no matter how much I mess up, often that seed will still sprout and grow. I love to just go sit with my coffee and feel like a bystander to the Gardener as He does His thing.

Father Gardener loves to give His good gifts in the form of seeds and then say, "Partner with Me! Let's go on an adventure!" We can receive the seed in the fertile soil of faith, with all the rocks cleared away. We get to envision His glory in the growth.

The seed that was our daughter was planted in our hearts before Steve and I ever married. Steve comes from a heritage of adoption. His grandfather, Haskell Chesshir, a missionary to South Korea, volunteered to help Harry and Bertha Holt as they were pioneering their first orphanage in South Korea in the 1950s. The Holts were dismayed at the overflow of mixed-blood orphans overflowing Korean hospitals, and after adopting eight orphans themselves, Harry and Bertha were trying desperately to get more orphans to waiting families in America. Haskell met Harry in downtown Seoul one day and saw the tears in his eyes as he talked about how he could not care for them because he couldn't process them quickly enough to get them out of the country before they would die. Besides needing housing for the children, Haskell had land on his mission compound that needed a building on it or the government was going to take it away. As a short-term solution, Haskell found old military trucks, and they made beds for the babies in the back of those trucks until they could build a little two-room shack, then another, until they could house up to 125 orphans at a time on his land. Housing being solved, another challenge was the bed situation. After the Korean War, the South had suffered so much damage that there weren't enough trees or wood to build cribs. Some of Haskell's own younger children had to sleep in dresser drawers during that postwar winter. Then at the young age of sixteen, Steve's mother, Jenetta, flew with three ill babies on a special chartered flight from Seoul, delivering them to their waiting families in the United States. Those tender-hearted missionaries saw precious orphans as worth saving, whatever it took.

Steve's mother, Jenetta, at age sixteen when she
took three babies to the U.S. for adoption

The Holt family actually began to change the face of international adoption with their aggressive determined love that would not take no for an answer. Up until then, adoption was a hush-hush thing where U.S. adoption agencies only matched families with children who looked like them so no one would know they were adopted. When the Holts brought obviously Asian children into American families, it began to challenge that idea of keeping adoptions secret. Shame began to melt and celebrating their adoptions suddenly became okay. By 1966, the Holts had established their adoption agency in the U.S. and more than 3,000 South Korean orphans had been placed in homes. Harry passed away in 1964 while in South Korea, but Bertha continued with the work, and in 1966 President Johnson named her National Mother of the Year, and was inducted into the National Women's Hall of Fame in 2002, two years after her death at age ninety-six. She has personally become one of my heroes. Steve's Aunt Sherry grew up with the Holt's daughter Molly and helped her care for the sick babies. Molly continues to this day to work in South Korea with children and adults with special needs.

I feel so honored to be a small part of a big family legacy that valued the orphan. The Chesshir family has continued in this legacy of adoption and has become a clan of many different races and ethnicities. I love going to the family reunions and seeing the rainbow of skin colors that have been adopted into this amazing lineage. So adoption seems to be in our blood, and it was something we always knew we wanted to do.

When Steve and I married, we believed the poem "The Road Not Taken" by Robert Frost would be our road map. We knew we did not want the typical American dream. Making the decision to be missionaries in Bangkok, Thailand, wasn't all easy, but it was filled with hope and expectancy for living lives that had eternal vision and purpose. However, traveling that path once our children came along felt a whole lot different. When we started to grow our family, it felt much more like Tolkien's hobbit Bilbo leaving the Shire. With each child—biological, foster, and adopted—we began to understand the sacrifice involved. The yes to Jesus became harder to give.

The Perfect Seeds

In the fall of 2001, God gave us the name of our next seed: Jezreel Pearl. Each of our children so far had his or her own miracle story. Bethany Hope, our first daughter, was our miracle lost at only four hours old. Our two-time miracle, Isaiah, was, I believe, resurrected in my womb. My doctor instructed me to come in after what appeared in all certainty to be a miscarriage. We lived in Bangkok, and our church was on the fifth floor of a row building. Climbing five flights in that hot, steamy hallway was exhausting and demanding on my body during the early stages of my pregnancy with Isaiah. One day, I went to church for a prayer service, and by the time I got to the top of those stairs, I was cramping and bleeding. Everything passing out of my body indicated that my baby was gone.

The pain and injustice of losing Bethany was still fresh, and I did not feel like praying, "Thy will be done." A warring spirit rose up in me as I went home, locked myself in my room, and began to worship. I did not know what travailing prayer was at that time, but from what I know now, that was it. I didn't pray that if something was wrong, God could take my baby. I prayed that if something was wrong, would He please fix it. That if my baby was dead, would He bring him back to life. I assumed that God gave life to sustain it, not steal it back. After my time in prayer, I went to bed feeling spent.

Since it was the weekend, I could not get in to see my doctor, so I decided to wait until Monday. My teammate, who was also pregnant, came to tell me how sorry she was about the miscarriage. When I told her I felt as if Isaiah were still alive somehow, I could read the pity on her face.

And yet, the next morning when I woke up, I knew something was different. I looked at myself in the mirror, and I saw my son's life in my own eyes. I knew he was alive! And so, on Monday morning when my doctor wanted to do an ultrasound to see if I needed a D&C, I knew what she would find. She was the only one surprised to see that beautiful heart beating on the screen. Then again at his birth, we almost lost him a second time. He came way too early—nothing would stop him. God had given us his name, Isaiah, which means "Jehovah Saves."

He was born all black and blue without a sound, rushing into this world only to make time stand still in that room. Memories of our Bethany flooded my vision, and Steve and I cried out his name "Jehovah Saves!" into the ticking noise of that Apgar clock. And finally, with a vomit of blood and water, his breath and cry came.

It was a year of miracles. We had joined with believers to fast and pray George W. Bush into the White House. Oh, how we celebrated when we watched him go to church on his first day of office to worship and pray for the nation. We hoped he might be the one that would end abortion in our America. Even though we labored in Thailand church planting, our hearts also groaned for our home country and the slaughter of innocent babies.

Yes, it had been a year of miracles but an exhausting one as well. After a month in the NICU, Isaiah was able to come home. But raising a preemie was not something our doctor prepared us to do. He cried any time we went out. He was inconsolable at worship, parties, and the grocery store. No one told us all his senses were still not developed, and he wouldn't be able to handle such stimulation.

Isaiah was definitely a challenge, but he was only nine months old when the Lord began speaking to us about Jezreel.

The Perfect Soil

In this season of miracles, hope was restored. With Isaiah nearing his first birthday, I read 1 Kings 13, where dead bones came back to life. On Thanksgiving Day in 2001, I wrote in my journal:

Elisha did miracles even after he died because of God's Spirit on him! I want that much of God's Spirit! Give me more Lord! Fill me to overflowing so that TRUE LIFE spills out of me wherever I go! Living Waters, spring up in me! Banish all fear! Speak to me—may Your voice be loud and clear . . . Prepare my body and everything else for our next child. I believe her name will be Jezreel.

A couple weeks later, to my dismay, I thought I was pregnant again. I cried and felt so overwhelmed and then guilty at the same time for not wanting another child. When my cycle finally began, I was so relieved. But our hearts began to wonder what Jehovah Sneaky was doing. We didn't know it at the time, but that was when Jezreel was actually being born in a small village in northern China. It was as if when she entered this physical world from the heavens, her spirit traveled to the womb of my spirit and planted herself there. That "pregnancy" I was sensing was that of life growing within that every mother knows. And that life was my adopted daughter, Jezreel Pearl.

So life grows. When the soil of our heart is fertile and has been tended, God can grow the most amazing, exotic beauty that will spread His glory and fragrance. The glory of "the seed" is that we can receive this heavenly DNA and see it replicated and multiplied here on earth, if we so choose. The prophet Hosea wrote of the glory of the planting:

> "In that day I will respond," declares the Lord—"I will respond to the skies, and they will respond to the earth; and the earth will respond to the grain, the new wine and the olive oil, and they will respond to Jezreel. I will plant her for myself in the land; I will show my love to the one I called 'Not my loved one.' I will say to those called 'Not my people,' 'You are my people'; and they will say, 'You are my God.'" (Hosea 2:21–23)

What seed could be more beautiful than the one that brings forth human life in the glory and image of God? King David sang, "God sets the lonely in families" (Psalm 68:6). He is always about this business because of who He is as a good Father "who provided for the poor" (verse 10) and "daily bears our burdens" (verse 19). My prayer is that you will choose to join Him in this business of family. That you would let your home and heart become a place where fertile soil is available for Him to plant and bring forth another life to safely grow.

Jezreel Pearl, age sixteen

Open Arms

In my heart I see
Their faces
Living in faraway places
My heart unlocked
My arms are open
A home, and love and
God to hope in
These are things that I can do
His strength and care will
See me through.

I woke up in the morning

With so much on my plate.
I need to stop and sit
With God, but I'm already
Running late.

I stop and pause and take
A breath
His peace will fill my
Day instead.
And so I pray and
Praise and sing before
I leave my bed.

He greets me with such
Love and grace
As I gaze with awe
Into His face.
I feel Him prying
At my heart
He's cracked it open
Wide apart.

For children that are without
A home,
"But Lord, mine
Are fully grown!"

My daughter, I greet
You daily with my song.
In my arms you
Belong.
These little ones they are

Mine too.

There's so much that you

Can do.

—*"Open Arms" by Jo Carman*

'VE MOVED AROUND A LOT in my life, and I have found there are generally two kinds of people: those with open arms and those with closed arms. I can vividly picture Jesus when He asked the children to come to Him. I'm sure His arms were wide open to beckon and invite them, reassuring them that His love would encircle them in safety. I love to imagine them running to be first to jump on His lap, smooching His cheeks, hanging from His limbs, and whispering secrets in His ears. This is one of my favorite mental pictures of Jesus, because I am one of those kids and because it is such a distilled essence of who the Father is.

When I visit a home or a church for the first time, I can feel the arms. The church with arms folded is such a sad reflection of Father God. It's one that needs to get to know you first, or your stuff, to see if you have it under control or not. The church with open arms is the one that makes you feel loved and accepted as you walk in. It is a posture that speaks welcome. When you open your arms to someone, the most vulnerable part of you is open, literally and figuratively. When you open your arms wide you say, "Come feel my love. Come hurt me. Bring your arrows and your blades to the most tender parts of me. It's okay. Father will help us work this out." This embrace will surely be accompanied by blood, pain, and tears.

It's a scary way to live. It feels easier to keep my arms to myself. It might seem like it's actually more about people's personalities rather than posture. But biblically speaking, I don't think Jesus gives us much of a choice on this. He compared Himself to a hen gathering "her chicks under her wings" (Matthew 23:37). He lived in such a way that let others wound Him for the sake of love. And then He declared, "Very truly I tell you, whoever believes in me will do the works I have been doing, and they will do even greater things than these, because I am going to the Father" (John 14:12).

Even greater? Here is another passage that we can't just say, "Huh... wonder what that means?" We have to say, "Wow! What in this world is 'greater things'? What in the world are those things? I want them!" I am no theologian, but God's Word says the greatest thing we can do is love. As a witness to the supernatural power of love in an adoption, I can confidently say that adoption could be one of those great works He's talking about. At its very root, adoption describes God's love. It is a love that gets up and leaves a majestic throne—or a La-Z-Boy in our case—and goes out. It is a love that fills us so fully that we absolutely have to find someone to overflow onto. It's a love that says, "I have so much love, and this love that's been freely given to me is too extravagant to keep to myself." We are the Cinderellas at the ball, and now we get to invite the others to our feast. And we can offer all the resources of heaven that are at our disposal.

The Decision

When we made our decision to adopt, we had a healthy, full family of seven. We did not feel a lack or an emptiness around our table. I would look at my husband every day and thank the Lord for what a good father he was because I knew good fathers are hard to find. But I knew there was room at our table. I used to wonder, after having two or three kids, how you could love them all or even make time for them all. We certainly weren't perfect parents, but we were growing more and more aware of God's provision as we kept putting more demands on heaven. The resources just multiplied and never ran out. With that understanding, we could look at a child with overwhelming needs and know heaven is on our side and nothing is too great for Him. We were definitely naive to just how much beyond ourselves we would stretch, but I think that's the case with anything worth doing.

We began our adoption in Bangkok. As I weighed the gravity of adopting a stranger into our family, I asked the Lord for counsel. I had seen some adopted children grow up in good, loving homes and end up rebelling and bringing grief upon grief to their families. I feared risking the safety of our happy little home. And so we asked Him to speak.

The Messengers

Right before we finished our application, some old friends from the States came to visit us in Bangkok. I was excited because I knew that family had several biological children and an adopted one. They were a great family with godly, happy kids, and I had a lot of respect for them. After the kids were in bed, we listened to their adoptive journey. They shared all the God stories you always hear with adoptions, all the miracles. But then one parent shared the hard stuff.

The successes and resilience of their amazing family seemed to magnify the slowness and weakness of this new one. They were brutally honest with their doubts and misgivings. I was dumbfounded and heartbroken to see that deep of a struggle that far into their journey with their son. Later that night, Steve and I struggled as we talked in bed of what God was saying. He had obviously brought them to us halfway across the world as a voice in a strategic time, but what was the message?

I just couldn't believe it was the Lord saying not to do it. We didn't have many answers at that time, but we finally told ourselves that love is a choice and love is a risk. And we jumped off another scary cliff of comfort and said yes. This family's story would come back to haunt me years later when I contemplated whether or not we ourselves had made a mistake and I was plagued by self-doubt. I wondered if I actually just didn't want to hear what God was saying through them.

Yes or No?

We chose to shelve our doubts and went on to finish our application, praying and seeking God the entire way. The adoption agency we used had this question on their application:

Are you open to considering a child with special needs? Yes _____ No _____. There was no "maybe" box to check.

There was no box for "If God tells me to."

Just "yes" or "no," and you had to check one. Looking back on it, that was quite clever of them.

As you can imagine, we prayed some more. We decided we needed a couple of weeks to answer that question. I was ashamed to admit, the thought of adopting a special-needs child had never even crossed my mind. I was so thankful for the gorgeous, healthy, biological children we had. Why go asking for intentional hardship? Why indeed? Our lives as missionaries already had what I thought was a good amount of hardship.

And yet, during those two weeks, children with special needs seemed to come out of the woodwork everywhere we went. I'm convinced that God purposely brought those families my way. Beautiful families with deaf children, children with Down syndrome, and with intellectual disabilities all of a sudden showed up on my radar. I had never considered that we might get promoted to join that community of not just parents but super heroes.

During that time of prayer, we went to the beach for a few days of rest. I'll never forget sunning by the pool when I suddenly looked up to see what looked like an angel. This tall, handsome Scandinavian man was carrying an Indian boy who must have been at least nine or ten years old. But it looked effortless for this father. He so tenderly carried him around the pool, pointing out a waterfall, the café, and the kids' pool. The man's blond hair gleamed so bright in the sun in contrast to his son's dark skin that it glowed. I was smitten at this beauty. He finally came over to his wife to sit down, and she was holding a Thai baby on her lap. Since I was staring unashamedly, I thought I might as well introduce myself. I found out that this lovely family had just adopted their second child from Thailand.

God was showing off His children and parents to me in order to give us our answer. I could never refuse a child from my own body; how could we choose the right child to join our family? Only God can do that, and I knew we could trust Him in His decision. We checked the "yes" box and sent the application off to the adoption agency. Fear and hesitation were not absent. I closed my eyes to them, and we forged ahead in to the goodness of God.

Sacrificial Love

Looking back now, I realize the decision was so hard because it meant volunteering for sacrifice. Sacrifice seems to be at the end of every love road, or at least a very significant stop along the way. I am amazed when reading in the Bible about Hannah's sacrifice of her child, Samuel. She had prayed and pined for this child for lonely years, but her Magnificat, her song of praise recorded in 1 Samuel 2:1–10 after she returned him to the temple, is compared to Mary's, the mother of Christ, after her angelic visitation. Hannah's prophetic prayer is full of praise and joy, not bitterness. True sacrifice because of love brings pain, but with it also overwhelming joy.

In a particularly difficult season with Jezreel, I felt like sacrifice was all I was doing every day. It seemed my selfish self died a fresh death every single day to serve this daughter. I am one of those essential-oils moms. I love to clean with them, perfume with them, and even cook with them. My favorite one is one of the most expensive: frankincense. I love the smell, and I love that it was a gift brought to Jesus upon His arrival here on earth. One day I took Jezreel into my bathroom, and I took a whole new bottle of that frankincense oil and anointed her as an offering, repenting to the Lord again for selfishness and committing to love and serve her to the best of my ability. She laughed and hugged me, having no clue about what was really happening in the transaction.

In writing this book, we are now fifteen years into our love journey with Jezreel. In that same journey, our family entered into one of its most challenging seasons. Almost five years ago, my husband, Steve, was diagnosed with ALS, also known as Lou Gehrig's disease. As we have groaned under the weight of this illness, we have had to purposely fix our eyes on Jesus. Love has demanded sacrifices we never dreamed we would have to make. More layers of my selfishness have surfaced. We try not to spend a lot of time thinking about the sacrifices but rather meditate on gratitude for what we do have. Serving Steve in his weakness is a holy thing. I get to know Christ's sacrifice in a very small way. Christ's love for His family compelled Him to volunteer for sacrifice and suffering.

I believe this is where love shines its brightest. A life poured out like Mary of Bethany's perfume is a fragrant offering to the Lord (John 12:3). Sacrifice is a hallmark of true love.

Nineteenth century missionary and artist Lilias Trotter, who ministered to young underprivileged girls in London, has long been an inspiration to me. Her poem has become my daily prayer:

Measure thy life by loss and not by gain,
Not by the wine drunk, but by the wine poured forth,
For love's strength standeth in love's sacrifice,
And he who suffers most has most to give.

Don't get me wrong; I don't believe we were given Steve's dreaded disease to test our love. We actively contend for his healing and believe that Jesus offered His back for it. But while we wait and contend, we pray our love does not fail but reflects His love. I can relate facing a terminal diagnosis with no known cure to the zoom lens on a camera. What is most important this side of eternity gets to stay in the foreground. And when you can face death squarely and not flinch, a lot of other things get clearer. Adventure journalist Hunter S. Thompson's quote is one of our favorites: "Life is not a journey to the grave with the intention of arriving safely in a pretty and well-preserved body, but rather to skid in broadside, thoroughly used up, and proclaiming, 'Wow! What a ride!'"

Our earthly life is so short compared to our eternal one. The sacrifices we make here with our time, money, and energy matter so little when we think of the eternal joy set before us. What will matter most when we stand before the Lord on our Judgment Day is what we did with our resources. The question at hand will be, did we let our pitcher of life get poured out as our offering? Or were we more like water fountains, dispensing our life here and there to quench some thirst, yet retaining most of the water still inside?

It's a good thing we snapped a picture that day when we signed our papers and jumped in with both feet to adopt. I barely recognize those two people anymore.

Nothing to Fear

"Feed your faith and your fears will starve to death."
—Unkown

F EAR IS OFTEN AT THE root of all our reasons for not adopting, fostering, or even signing up for childcare on a Sunday. Fears of sleepless nights, drained resources, not locking the knife drawer, and, especially, our own inadequacies and doubts in our parenting ability. We picture their adorable faces, but we have heard the horror stories. We think maybe we could somehow make a difference in the life of a child, but then all of a sudden some demon from hell comes and vomits up every past mistake right at our feet. He sneers at us and tells us to have a good look. We stare and start to mop it up, agreeing with how the filth stinks and how true those accusations are: "We can't do such a noble thing as save a human life"; "I am unworthy, impatient, selfish, and short-tempered." Saying yes to a child is a life-altering decision for you and the child. In fact, we don't truly know what we are saying yes to. What in the world might be behind those big eyes or buried deep in that young heart? We have no way of knowing.

I was afraid of so many things when we answered yes. As an inexperienced young missionary, I had already dealt with some fears. Bugs, rats, scorpions, tropical diseases, and the fear of flying were among a few that came with the mission field. Many times I had to step outside my sheltered self and act in a way that was in direct opposition to that fear. My husband, Steve, says, "There's the facts, and then there's truth. God's truth always trumps the facts." I was learning to walk in God's truth consistently, not just when I wasn't afraid. My first Sunday in Bangkok felt quite intimidating to this little girl from the shire. My heart wanted to be a missionary and serve Him there, but every other part of me wanted to run away and hide. As we took communion that day, I couldn't understand a single word being spoken in Thai, but the Holy Spirit spoke to me, clear as a bell, "My righteous one will live by faith. And I take no pleasure in the one who shrinks back" (Hebrews 10:38).

"No pleasure"? All I wanted to do was to please Him. And so I wept and repented. And I made a decision that day that I have done my best to honor ever since: I will make no decision out of fear. When faced with financial struggles, health crises, or life directions, I will look at that situation with X-ray vision to see where the fear is hiding and step aside into the truth. It seems that the older I get, the bigger the decisions become. Often the scene from the movie *The Last of the Mohicans* comes to me in which Alice has just seen the man she loves, Col. Munro, brutally murdered at the hands of Magua, the enemy Huron chief. She moves to the edge of the cliff and everything moves in slow motion as the music crescendos. She looks down to her death and then back to her evil captor and then down the cliff again. It is a defining moment. She ultimately chooses the cliff. One can argue that she made the courageous decision by ending her life, but something in me wants to step away from the "cliff" when I am faced with fear. She jumped to her death, but instead I just want to turn away, to shrink back. Things seem to go in slow motion when fear paralyzes.

But I have another, much greater fear. I picture the day that Jesus, not my enemy, is in front of me. The day that my Savior, who gave it all, stands before me. On that day, what excuse could there be for shrinking back? What could hold up in front of such love and sacrifice but my very best? And then He'll open my book and read it aloud. I fear facing the undone assignments written in heaven for me. I fear seeing the gifts with my name on them marked "Return to Sender." I long for His pleasure now as well as on that day more than anything.

At the end of the day, what is there to fear in caring for Jesus' children? We may think that when we come to the end of ourselves, there is only barren wasteland. We can't believe the lies of this world that are telling us we're not enough, that once we reach the end of our resources it'll still not be enough. The end of ourselves, where we are unable to fix, help, be strong, or even take a step forward, is where God meets us. The truth is, the sooner we reach that place, the more opportunity there is to see miracles. The beauty of this life actually exists where God would like us to hang out. At the end of ourselves there are green pastures and still waters. That mysterious end of self is actually anything but a wasteland. It does feel like a death that you decide. But don't fear the end of your resources in all weakness; rejoice when you hit that joyful place because it is a place of true encounter with God!

Chosen

All my fears did not scuttle away once we signed and put that adoption application in the mail. When we decided to adopt a child with special needs, we were naive and unqualified. We didn't even feel qualified to choose our own child. One morning, not too long after we had turned in all our paperwork, I woke up with this passage filling my heart: "Let the morning bring me word of your unfailing love, for I have put my trust in you" (Psalm 143:8). I felt Holy Spirit's excitement as I ran to turn on the computer and open my email. My heart was racing because I knew my child was on that list. We knew we wanted a little girl from China, but after that we asked the Lord to show us which one was ordained as ours. We printed out all the girls' names on that list with their pictures and biographies. We gathered the family in our office, closed our eyes, and prayed that the Father would show us our daughter. Our oldest son, Michael, was nine years old at the time. With his eyes closed, he heard her Chinese name without even knowing what it was. Even Isaiah, who was just a toddler then, picked her picture off the floor and said, "Let's try this one!"

I'm grateful that God clearly spoke to us about which little girl was ours. In the picture, she was a lost-looking girl with boyish hair, and you could see someone's arm helping her stand up for the picture. Her bio said her special need was a "congenital heart disease." At that time we knew there were heart surgeries for that sort of thing. We wouldn't learn just how many special needs she had until much later.

Our yes to Jezreel seemed to set numerous things into motion— or orbit rather. As soon as we responded to the orphanage with our choice, they told us we actually could not adopt her; she was too ill. They wouldn't tell us what was wrong. She had been abandoned at the orphanage when she was two years old. Apparently, when the orphanage realized the severity of her disease, they planned to place her in one of their dying rooms and let her die. I'm sure the heart surgery was too expensive for her parents as well as the orphanage. But because of Steve's family connections in Asia, we were able to issue a request from a heart hospital in central China that she be brought to their clinic and examined. She was released from the orphanage for that trip under the impression that repairing her heart might make her more adoptable, and it was paid for by the clinic. Unbeknownst to the orphanage, we were finally able to find out what her diagnosis was from our friends. What they told us was quite overwhelming.

We knew that at three years old, she still could not walk or talk. They told us she had only one ventricle in her heart and that she was blue from lack of oxygen. Children born with this abnormality usually have surgery as newborns to begin the correction. The clinic that examined Jezzie contacted Love Without Boundaries, an organization that helps children like Jezreel get the surgeries they need so they can be more readily adopted. After a lot of prayer, we learned she was to go back with her nanny to the same heart clinic for her first surgical procedure, paid for by Love Without Boundaries. After the surgery, the orphanage changed their minds and said we could adopt her after all.

After pushing through the fears of not having what it would take to raise Jezreel, other fears were waiting in the wings to take their place. Finances were quite a big issue, especially for my husband, Steve, as he felt such a strong responsibility to provide for his family. As missionaries, we saw provisional miracles often, and we were never in lack. While we did not have a lot budgeted for savings, we did set up college funds for our children. Our first financial fleece was the required five thousand dollar up-front deposit. Right at the time we needed it, someone sent us five thousand dollars out of the blue for no particular reason. We were encouraged to move forward, taking the money as God's partnership to do what we could not do ourselves. We expected the adoption itself to probably exceed thirty thousand dollars, not including medical costs, home-study plane fare, and on and on. One day, Steve was driving home from his time with the Lord at a local park. He told God the obvious: we did not have that money. God replied, *Yes, you do.* And Steve knew better than to argue with Him. The only money we had, to speak of, were the college funds we set up for our biological children. Our oldest son, Michael, had the most in his account, but it was still not enough to cover all we would need.

After Steve returned home, we talked and prayed, eventually feeling that money was our loaves and fishes to give to the Multiplier. We have been blown away by just how many times He has multiplied those few thousand dollars. So we knew we could trust the Lord for Michael's college education. The adoption went on to cost well over thirty thousand dollars when all was said and done. We ended up traveling to China to get Jezreel at the most expensive time of year, when hotels triple in price. We also had to pay the plane fare for a social worker to come all the way to Thailand to do our home study. Not to mention, Jez has had numerous medical expenses, the largest being her open-heart surgery that totaled more than a million dollars without insurance. And yet, we have never gone into debt for those expenses. We have had front-row seats in the theater of God's goodness, watching the Father's love spare no expense for His precious one.

Years later, as our son Michael finished high school and we were planning for college, our family was in the lowest place financially we have ever been. We were back in the States, and after a difficult business venture we were unemployed and on food stamps. It was a humbling time. We never went hungry, but we had no money to send our firstborn to university. We reminded the Lord of the seed we had sown and asked Him to remember. We had spent that little bit of money we had on something dear to the Father, and now trusted Him with something dear to us. After being offered a meager scholarship at an expensive Christian university, Michael applied to a private Christian school closer to our Tennessee home. He was offered a full ride, and by the end of his fifth year he had two degrees and was basically being paid to go to college. We can never out-give God, and He does nothing halfway.

Scary Special Needs

But what about those scary special needs? When Jezreel's broken heart was repaired and life became some form of normal, I just knew she would begin walking and talking and blooming in her new home. But she didn't. We would say "Mama" and would respond with "Ahhh." She would listen to me speak and even seem to understand, but she could not mimic my speech in any way that sounded remotely the same. Her tiny feet didn't even seem like they were made for walking. She would cry buckets of tears when we tried to get her to walk. I asked her doctor to examine her feet. Surely they had overlooked some foot deformity that made walking painful or not possible at all. He said nothing was wrong with her feet. Every day I kept asking the Lord for some instruction manual because even though we were loving Jezreel and she was loving us back, not much else seemed to be working. He seemed silent, and we felt clueless.

Since Jezreel was left at the orphanage when she was two years old, her past has remained a mystery to us. When we brought her home on the day of what they estimated was her fourth birthday, we didn't know what was wrong, much less how to fix it. And so as a family we began a journey of discovery. I continually reminded the Lord I was not a special ed teacher, therapist, doctor, nurse, or minister of deliverance. We did not even have much of a track record of successfully casting out demons, if that was what we were dealing with. I asked Him so many, many times why He chose me to be her mother. I told God He had made a mistake. What was He thinking? That I was superwoman? Supermom? When was He actually going to help me? Where was *my* therapist?

For Jezreel to survive her difficult beginnings, persevere through her thirteen-hour open-heart surgery, and all the recovery that would follow, God gifted her with a strong will to survive. It's very strong indeed. Many others look at her and marvel. As her mom, I daily beg the Lord for mercy. As a family, we have learned how to love Jezzie. How to understand her pain, help her, and champion her. We have learned to intercede for miracles and not give up when days turn into years. We have learned how not to revolve the whole family's lives around her. Like all our children, she is another planet in our orbit around our Sun, Jesus.

6

Bethany Hope

Steve Allen

I AM THE FATHER OF SEVEN children. I believe my main calling while on earth is to father—my birth children and spiritual children.

I believe unequivocally in the sanctity of life, the protection of the unborn, and the right to life for those who have no voice, but there was a time that the spirit of fear led me to partner with death. I know firsthand that sometimes the line between life and death is unclear. During the writing of this book, twenty-four years after our daughter Bethany was born, the Holy Spirit convicted me again of life and Him as its only Author.

As a young missionary in Bangkok, Thailand, my wife, Samantha, had significant complications during her pregnancy with our second child. It had been an unexpected pregnancy just ten months after our first child, Michael, was born. Early on, nine out of ten doctors at our hospital told us to abort, that continuing the pregnancy could endanger Sam's life, and that the baby would probably not live anyway. We told them we could not do that and chose to trust God with our baby. Our doctor was unsupportive of our decision, so we found a new doctor, the only Christian obstetrician we knew of in the city. Samantha had one scary episode where she had to be hospitalized, and the doctor said Sam would most certainly miscarry. That is when the Lord gave Sam our baby's name—Bethany Hope—and knowledge she was a girl. Though we went home with that baby still alive and kicking in Sam's womb, it was a difficult pregnancy. Friends and family all over the world began to pray for Sam and Bethany. Sam was instructed to stay flat on her back at all times, and friends and family had to take turns helping us take care of Michael and Sam. At only twenty-six weeks into the pregnancy, Samantha went into premature labor and was rushed to the hospital.

Rushed was not really the word. I was in downtown Bangkok, and because of traffic, I could not get home in time to take Sam. That meant our teammates had to carry her down the stairs in a chair and take her to the hospital across town. The rainy season had begun and Bangkok streets were flooded so traffic was worse than usual. I met them at the hospital, and after a difficult breech delivery, our Bethany was born. She was placed not into our arms but into an incubator along with numerous tubes, monitors, and a lung machine.

Sam was whisked away without getting to see Bethany, as she had begun an infection that had to be treated immediately. They told me that at twenty-six weeks, Bethany was too premature and showed me a scan of her underdeveloped brain. She was hooked up to a lung machine at its lowest level, and the pediatrician said if they increased the air flow any more her underdeveloped lungs would burst. He said that if she somehow did live, she would never be normal.

The neonatal specialist and Sam's obstetrician told me it was best to turn off the life-support machine since she probably would not live. We had great respect for this Christian doctor, as she had agreed to fight and pray with us for Bethany's life. She did not suggest we include Sam in this decision because I think she knew what Samantha would say. Thinking that I was doing the best for Samantha and my family, and out of fear, I agreed with the two doctors, and they turned off her lung machine. And Bethany was gone.

I then went back to the room and told Samantha that Bethany had already gone to heaven. I did not tell her about the choice I had been given or the brain scan they had done.

For twenty-four years I kept that secret to myself.

Over the years, I've justified my decision that I was protecting Sam and my family, doing the best for them and for Bethany.

This past fall, during a strategic prayer focus with our prayer community for the midterm elections, the Supreme Court, and for the rights of the unborn, the Holy Spirit began to gently speak to me to share with Samantha what happened on the day of Bethany's birth, March 23, 1994.

It was painful as I shared with Samantha that I had made the decision about Bethany without her and without praying together. She quietly listened and said she needed some time to process what I shared. Understandably, great anger rose up in her spirit, as she felt I had taken Bethany away from her, and she realized her doctor had lied to her. Grieving Bethany twenty-four years before was the most painful thing we had been through as a young family, sending us back to the States for a time of marriage counseling and healing. After Bethany's death, her doctor had asked to do an autopsy to try to determine her cause of death. We wanted to know also, so we agreed. Sam saw her brain scan for the first time at her postpartum, post-autopsy appointment, with her doctor falsely indicating the scan was done during the autopsy, and not before her death. This new knowledge for Samantha teleported us back to those painful days as if they'd happened only yesterday.

Over the next few weeks after I had shared with Sam, with the covering, counsel, and prayers of spiritual fathers, mothers, and our best friends, we walked through that pain together. So much grace has covered both of us. I believe God brought this up during the writing of this book, not just for us, or for Bethany, but also for you the reader. I share this to be transparent as an imperfect father who has learned the heart of the heavenly Father in this life's most fragile and vulnerable moments. He alone is the Author of life, and only He is worthy to decide its beginning and its end. As I fight a terminal diagnosis myself, I have determined that my doctors do not have the say over my life and death. That belongs only to the Lord, and I believe His plan is always for our good and to manifest His glory. We cannot presume we know any better.

We will never know this side of heaven if Bethany would have lived and what miracles God might have done, because we did not give Him the opportunity. We do know she is in the great cloud of witnesses now, forgiving, loving, and praying for us. She is cheering me on as I run my race and I prove all my doctors wrong. Life is beautiful, and just the opposite is true too: death before its time is ugly, and the direct antithesis of His design. Even in the darkest of moments and most difficult of circumstances, when it seems that life will be or should be extinguished, we must trust it to God. He is the only One big enough for our most paramount life-and-death decisions.

Ungodly Alliances
Samantha

I just returned from the 2019 March for Life rally in Washington, DC. It was my first one, though not my first time to stand in front of the Supreme Court with "LIFE" tape over my mouth while praying silently for the unborn and for Roe v. Wade to be overturned. At the end of the march, women standing on the steps in front of our nation's highest court shared their tearful testimonies. Some mothers who had aborted their babies and suffered in silence were just now deciding to share the kind of hell they had suffered. Some testimonies were from women who were abortion survivors. One woman in particular was born right at the same gestational age as Bethany, twenty-six weeks. Like Bethany, doctors told her mother that her baby would never live, and if she somehow did, she would never be normal. Her mother threatened to sue the abortionist if he went ahead and killed her baby, and her baby went on to live and thrive and tell us how thankful she was for her mother's choice to fight for life, even at the very last moment.

I couldn't help but think of Bethany again and weep. What testimonies would she have given? What miracles would God have done in her life had we chosen differently?

On the plane home, I opened my Bible to 2 Chronicles 20–21. In that passage a vast army was coming against Jehoshaphat, king of Judah. In Jerusalem at the temple of the Lord in front of all Judah, King Jehoshaphat, along with all the men, women, and children, beseeched the Lord for help. Not only did the Lord help them, they didn't even have to fight on that day.

Jehoshaphat told them that when they showed faith in the Lord and His prophets, they would be successful. Not only were they successful, but they went home with more plunder than they could carry. More than they had asked for. But soon after, King Jehoshaphat made an alliance with the evil king of Israel, Ahaziah, and a door of evil was opened that ushered in more evil than Jehoshaphat could have imagined. His son not only murdered all of his brothers, but he married a daughter of the evil King Ahab. Generations to come would pay for his sin that just continued to mushroom and multiply.

When we were in Washington, DC, for the march, we also joined a justice meeting with a local house of prayer. As we prayed for the ending of abortion in America, we talked about how the Awaken the Dawn tent gatherings today in all the capital cities of America just might be a redemptive pleasure to the Lord in light of compromise years ago. In the revival tent meetings of the 1920s, Margaret Sanger, the founder of Planned Parenthood, offered finances to those hosting the revivals if she could put her own tent with her birth control teachings in front. Many agreed.

What an unholy alliance that was, and what evil rushed in that generations now are paying for. What might have happened if the church had stood unflinching and uncompromising, trusting only the Lord for the finances? What might have happened if the body of Christ had taken her place and believed God for the provision in faith?

God takes unholy alliances seriously because He expects more from His people. He knows we are weak and cannot fight our enemies on our own, but He does demand our trust. If compromise and unbelief are at the root of our decisions, He is not pleased and we will reap what we sow. What unholy alliances do we have with our culture today? If it's blatant heresy or a doctor's opinion that goes against what God had said, God holds us accountable to believe Him and to trust Him. He knows we are dust, and He said He will fight for us if we will only be still. But trust with no compromise is not optional.

God's grace is so abundant to cover our sin twenty-four years ago. We want to be transparent with it and let God redeem our past mistakes in His goodness. But we also want Bethany's voice to be heard. We understand so much more now about the power of one human life, and the miracle-working power of our God. We share our story so that even just one more person might decide to abandon fear and choose life.

7

The Heart of the Father

Steve Allen

ET ME TELL YOU ABOUT my own beloved father. My father was my hero. He passed away in March 2018 at the age of eighty-four after a six-year battle with Parkinson's. He was one of the most godly men I've ever known.

Sidney N. Allen was born and raised in the dusty, windswept West Texas town of Lubbock in the 1930s. His parents raised him to love God and His living Word. He learned the importance of integrity, keeping your word, a strong work ethic, and a good education.

As a teenager, I loved to watch my father, an elder in the church, interact with members on Sunday mornings or evenings after services. Members often came to him for counsel and encouragement. With profound patience and compassion he would quietly listen, often with a hand on their shoulder, and then speak words of wisdom and pray for them. Looking back, I now realize that my father was modeling the heart of our heavenly Father to us.

Dad also modeled a man who can be trusted. As author Stephen R. Covey wrote, "Relationship happens at the speed of trust." Equally quotable, Under Armour CEO Kevin Plank said, "Trust is gained in drops but lost in buckets." My father had the rare gift of holding buckets of trust. Everyone I knew trusted him. I believe that one of the reasons why people trusted him was because of his deep, authentic, genuine humility. It was the bedrock upon which his integrity stood.

As a tribute to my father's character, I shared this verse from the prophet Micah at my father's memorial: "He has shown you, O man, what is good; And what does the Lord require of you But to do justly, To love mercy, And to walk humbly with your God" (Micah 6:8, NKJV).

Act, Love, Walk = Action Verbs
Feet to Our Faith

Authentic Christianity
Justice, Mercy, Humility

These are foundational pillars of virtue that reflect the nature of God. My father had the exceptional character of displaying and modeling all three of these to all those he came in contact with. Thank you, Dad, for showing us the heart of the Father.

Three Primary Things

A father's role is to provide three primary things for his children: provision, protection, and identity.

My father did this for us in a simple and quiet yet profound way that, as I look back on my childhood, I'm so deeply grateful for. He did all three well, but the most important pillar of these is identity.

Identity is the essence of who we are and whose we are. On a daily basis, my dad modeled for us what it means to be a follower of Jesus and a son of the living God. One of the most impacting ways he did that was through his spiritual leadership in our family's morning devotions.

We grew up on the mission field in Seoul, South Korea, where we woke up early each morning to get ready for our downtown international school, about an hour away. My mom always had a hot breakfast waiting for us, and we'd eat together as a family while my dad led our morning devotions. We each had a large Good News Bible, illustrated with photos from the Holy Land, and took turns reading from it. Afterward, my father would lead us in prayer.

The faithfulness my father modeled to us was life transforming. Day after day, week after week, month after month, and year after year, he led us in those morning devotionals. I don't remember a particular devotional standing out, but his godly spiritual leadership, consistency, and faithfulness still resonates in my heart today. The apostle Paul wrote that "faith comes from hearing the message, and the message is heard through the word about Christ" (Romans 10:17), and our faith foundation was firmly established through Dad's daily ritual.

Epiphany

The first time I held my firstborn son, Michael, in my arms after his birth, I had an epiphany of the Father's love. I sensed I was on holy ground. It was as if I was encountering the love of God for the first time all over again. My spirit embraced a deeper dimension than I had ever experienced. In that moment knew the pure holy love God has for me.

As I felt that enormous love for my own son, it struck me that this is how my heavenly Father feels about me. I could suddenly "grasp how wide and long and high and deep is the love of Christ" (Ephesians 3:18) for me. And I understood that nothing, absolutely nothing, can "separate us from the love of God that is in Christ Jesus our Lord" (Romans 8:39). The nature of God is the love of God. We yearn to experience that love. We hunger to see His face.

In Scripture, Philip asked Jesus, "Lord, show us the Father" (John 14:8).

And Jesus responded to him, "Anyone who has seen me has seen the Father" (verse 9). We can know Him through God's Word because "the Son is the radiance of God's glory and the exact representation of His being, sustaining all things by His most powerful Word" (Hebrews 1:3).

When we come into true relationship with the Father we embrace His nature, His goodness, and His love. God truly is the "father to the fatherless, a defender of widows. . . . God sets the lonely in families" (Psalm 68:5–6). And as the living *ecclesia*, the family of God, it is our privilege and responsibility to take care of the orphan, the poor, and the marginalized. If we have really met the Father, we will reflect His heart to the world around us. Oh, God, change us, transform us, and make us like You!

Steve and Jezzie
A Father's love

Plus-One Thinking

There are few dreams quite as sacred
As to raise eternal souls
The weight of such a calling
None save God can ever know.
To spend your life in secret
With no words or applause
Is an all-consuming fire
Of self-denial and certain loss;
Though, it takes a seed first dying
To bring forth a fruitful vine,
And the daybreak and the dawning
Of your reward unveil with time.

To give up your life for another's
Is the Gospel's simple truth,
And none live out its message
With an ardor quite like you.
Your artwork is a living soul,
Your loving words a pen,
You tell immortal stories
Through your lineage and kin.
And every time you wipe a tear
Or clean a dirty dish,
You wage a timeless war without
On selfishness within.
You call forth knights of valor
Out of wild, hungry boys,
And crown young girls with noble grace
That gives them courage and a voice.
Writing history with your womb,
You keep the ancient tale unfolding,
Without your sacrifice there'd be
No new mankind to share His glory.
So thank you for the part you've played
In this story of the ages,
Because of you, there's beauty untold
Now scripted across its pages.

—"Mother" by Nicole Forber

Y OU MAY HAVE FIGURED OUT by now that this little book is my urgent appeal. I hope and pray it encourages you to first pray, then open your arms a little wider and consider adoption and foster care. The fact that more than 440,000 children are in the foster-care system is overwhelming. Satan loves for us to feel overwhelmed and helpless when we see his work. But it is the Lord who comes as a rushing river when we lift up His name over any situation. You may feel ordinary, but if you have the Spirit of the living God dwelling inside you, you are far from ordinary. You are a superhero with super powers. You have all of heaven on your side, and angels are just waiting to be commissioned. The most powerful thing you can do when you look at the problem is to remember the heart of the Father and pray. We want to call you to a new prayer initiative. There is a God-birthed prayer movement in America right now called Bound4LIFE. In it women proclaim their "silent siege" by covering their mouths with red tape with the word *LIFE* emblazoned on it and standing in front of courtrooms and abortion clinics to protest the murder of babies and plead for justice.

What if we just kept going? Scripture speaks of how the Lord has taken those names that are dear to Him and "engraved them on the palms of [his] hands" letting everyone know He will never forget them (Isaiah 49:16). What if we were to ask the Lord for the name of a child to write on our palm to remember in prayer?

The Strategy: Plus One

Here is our strategy. Just as God knows and cares for each sparrow and can number the hairs of our heads, He knows the names of each hurting child in the world, and He cherishes each one (Matthew 10:29–31; Luke 12:6–7). What if we asked Him for the name of just one child? Would He speak to us? Would He whisper a name to you if you asked? What if we refused to be paralyzed by the problem and took a baby step in prayer? It's just a little yes to begin, not a jump-off-the-cliff yes.

If you are willing to begin here and ask, Creative Father might speak in one way or another about a child He would like to gift to you in prayer. He might give you a picture or even just the gender. He might give you a dream or a specific name. It might even be someone you have already met. You can be sure that He will not be silent when it comes to his kids. Take a Sharpie or a pen and write the name of that child on your palm. If He doesn't give you a specific name, you might want to name the child yourself until He reveals more to you. Like your heavenly Father, speak tenderly over that child, and remember him or her. Keep his needs before the Lord and yourself. Keep your Sharpie with your Bible so that when it wears off, you can write it again and again. I call that plus-one thinking.

If every church in America adopted one child, there would be no orphans in our country.

What if every believer took just one child to adopt in prayer? The SAFA students pictured on the right have names on their hands, and they are on the journey to end the orphan crisis just by praying every day. Where could this strategy lead? We are looking for strategies that start local and go global with kingdom impact. That's why I love movies like *Pay It Forward*. In it, when a young boy is given an assignment to think of something to change the world and put it into action, he conjures the notion of paying a favor not back, but forward—repaying good deeds not with payback, but with new good deeds done to three new people. The boy's efforts to make good on his idea bring a revolution not only in himself but also in an ever-widening circle of people completely unknown to him. In the same way, we can take care of the problems in our own country and then start impacting other nations, as God has designed.

One of my favorite prayer stories is included in John Ortberg's book *If You Want to Walk on Water, You've Got to Get Out of the Boat*. Doug Coe, who has a ministry in Washington, DC, was discipling a new believer and teaching him about prayer. This man is called Bob in the book, and he was an insurance salesman. When Bob read in his Bible, "Ask whatever you will in my name, and you shall receive it," he ran to Doug to see if it was really true. Doug wanted to encourage

SAFA students with the names of children on their
hands that they are praying for

Bob in learning how to pray, so when Bob wanted to start praying for Africa, Doug said he should narrow it down to one country. Bob chose Kenya.

What Doug did after that is where the extraordinary began. He offered to pay Bob five hundred dollars if he prayed for Kenya every single day for six months and nothing happened. And if something extraordinary did happen regarding Kenya, Bob would have to pay Doug five hundred dollars. If he did not pray every day, the deal was off.

For a while, Bob prayed for Kenya and nothing seemed to happen. Then one day, he found himself sitting at a dinner with the head of a very large orphanage in Kenya. He was invited to go and tour the orphanage. From that first trip, door after door began to open for Bob in Kenya that ultimately led to an audience with the president of Kenya and the opportunity to pray for the selection of his cabinet. Here we see the far-reaching effects of one man's consistent prayer and how it changed a nation. Just one praying man.

I will not give five hundred dollars to each person who signs up to pray in this prayer strategy, but I can pretty much guarantee a return of miracles. And we would love to hear about them as they begin to happen. So please write to the address in the back of this book and tell us your stories.

I mentioned in my introduction that you might not yet have a heart for children. Sometimes we have to take a first step without the heart, and the heart will follow. Back when we were a young mission team deciding what country to go to, my heart burned for Africa. My team had already been on a trip around the world to thirteen different countries before I joined by marriage. When Steve and I began dating, his team was deciding between Uganda and Thailand. I just knew it would be Uganda, since I felt that was where God was calling me. But on our first big team meeting the location shifted, in one day, from Uganda to Thailand. I couldn't believe it. I didn't even know where Thailand was on the map. I had no Asian friends to speak of, and to my shame, I had absolutely no affections for Asians.

So I began to pray. I spent nine months praying for the Thai people and their nation before I actually traveled there for the first time. And when I went, I fell in love. I loved them so much I ached in the pit of my stomach. God knit me together so tightly with those beautiful people, I will never be the same.

When you begin with prayer, you take a situation out of your realm of impossibility and put it into God's realm of possibility.

When you begin with obedience to God's heart, not just His commands, you walk by faith and not by sight.

Not everyone can adopt or foster a hurting child. But everyone can love, and everyone can pray. Everyone has been given loaves and fishes to give. I hope fathers will read this book, but my heart goes out to mothers. Whether you have yet to birth physical children, God has made you with His heart and a womb to mother. It is in your DNA. A lonely, orphan child will touch your heart in a way you cannot explain and move you to mother.

I hope this strategy can give us a place to start. Praying for one child begins adoption where it needs to begin, in the heavenly Father's heart. And from there the possibilities are endless. So whether you are married or single, made to mother or father, our prayer is that you begin to pray. That is our baby step.

The prayer manual that follows comes with scriptures you can pray. I like to pray one chapter each day. They can be used in your own devotional time, family prayer time, and corporate times of prayer. I currently have the names of three children on my palm. God gave me their faces in a dream, and I know they are siblings. I have no idea where this praying for them will lead. Right now, I know we cannot adopt or foster these three, but I can visualize them at my really big table. In my heart there is a table where they already have a place to sit, but we have decided they are already adopted in prayer. They are covered by a family and not left as orphans. The greatest miracle of all—life—is sure to follow.

Our family in 2017: (Back) Michael, Isaiah, Samantha, Steve, Kanaan, (front) Tirza, Jezreel, and Southern

9

Jezreel's Book

OUR JEZZIE IS SEVENTEEN YEARS old at the writing of this book. As soon as I began writing, she decided she wanted to write a book also, and she has been steadily writing for weeks. After we moved off the mission field back to the States, Jezreel was five and was ready to begin school. The school officials wanted to test her to see if she would qualify for special services. They told me in that meeting that Jezreel was "retarded." Evidently, that was when they still used such an archaic term. They told me the most that Jez would probably be able to do on her own was to learn to zip up her own pants and button her own buttons. They said I should not expect any more than that.

When we moved from California to Tennessee a year later, the

Individualized Education Program—the I.E.P. team as they called it—
at her new school reviewed the diagnosis. Not yet having even met
Jezreel they asked, "Would you like us to change that diagnosis to say
'developmental delay' on her records?"

More tears streamed for all these teachers I was meeting for the
first time. They seemed to understand a bit more about intelligence
and how it's measured. Other than required testing by the school, I
did not get Jezreel tested again until she was fifteen. In Nashville, we
went to a highly qualified child psychologist at Vanderbilt Hospital
who gave her the official label of "Severe Intellectual Disability." After
extensive testing, she told me that out of a hundred children in a
classroom, Jezreel's IQ was so low that she was not even knocking on
the door of that classroom. She told me that she was not even at the
front of the line outside the door of that classroom, but she would be
the last one in that line.

You can imagine how that makes a mama feel. I thanked her and
I told her I always knew Jezreel was one in a million.

What I know about intelligence is that it's extremely difficult to
measure. There are so many different types of smart. Jezreel loves God
and has given her life to Jesus. She spends time in His Word every
day. When we pray at breakfast for the unreached people groups of
the world, she prays for them to know all the fruit of the Holy Spirit.
She quotes her vision statement every morning because her daddy is
a leadership coach. She loves and forgives better than almost anyone I
know. I call that smart. She knows how your day is going without you
ever speaking a word. She knows how to worship without inhibition.
She can get up on time for school every single day without an alarm.
She really likes good food, a good fire, and a hot cup of tea. Family
means everything to her. I think she's got the most important stuff
right.

Turn Back Moments

When I signed up to be her mom, I signed up to be her champion. I had no idea it would be this hard. There are days I wish I could do it all over again and choose the easier road. On one of the worst of those days, I called my best friend and told her that maybe I should have listened to those friends that came from across the world. Maybe that was really God trying to tell us not to do it. And she said something I will never forget. She said, "Sam, you caught them in the middle of their journey. We all want to turn back when it gets hard. I'll bet he wouldn't say that now."

Now that is truth. Like Frodo when he told Gandalf that he wished the ring had never come to him, the middle of hard is just hard. But it doesn't mean we turn back or give up, or even that we made the wrong choice. It just means that the right choice is usually hard. But there is a prize for those who stick with it and don't give up. We will see miracles.

And here, at the end of my book, as we are about to go to print, a small miracle happened. I have not seen that family I just mentioned since that day in our home in Bangkok fourteen years ago. They had never met Jezreel or had any idea at all how much their transparency and vulnerability impacted our lives. But a couple weeks ago they came in town for a wedding. They bought us Thai food and we sat around our dining table talking and praying for over three hours. Their adopted son had tragically just passed away the month before at twenty-eight years old. We cried with them and talked more about the miracles and the hardships that come with this sacred journey of adoption. With their son newly back to heaven, they literally had just ended their physical journey with him. I desperately wanted to hear what they had to say from the finish line. I knew it was no coincidence that they were here now, sharing the end of their journey in the same humble and beautifully transparent way. I knew that what they had to share was important for all of us to hear.

Their feelings reminded me of Horton the Elephant's feelings when he was hatching that egg. It was an uncomfortable unnatural process; certainly not plan A. They often doubted themselves and their decision. God's miracles were obvious from the money provided to bring him home, to how he found his birth mom in a city of three million people, to how he accepted Christ three weeks before his death. Their hearts were broken yet full at the same time. It was hard and messy. On the phone last night, we joked about how our views on nature versus nurture had changed because of our kids. (Jezreel's intellectual disability made the simple task of learning how to tie her shoes take years, yet we never had to show her how to use chopsticks! She just knew.)

So my reflections continue on the plan B theme. Since the Garden of Eden, humans have been messing up God's plan A, and Father God's unrelenting merciful love works plan B like beauty from ashes. He is Redeemer, and His love for His children is stronger than our ruined plans. Adoption might feel like plan B, and in many ways it is. But there is no doubting the breathtaking, awe-inspiring love that pursues us when we fail at plan A. Look at Moses. God certainly didn't want all those Hebrew babies to die. But what a life Moses went on to lead! Numbers 12:3 says he was the most humble man on the earth. Could knowledge of his own adoption have had anything to do with his humility? The Bible seems to imply that it was this very humility that led Moses to such great intimacy with God.

So for every day I have breath, I am committed to our young lady to be her biggest fan to the finish line of our journey together. I yell the loudest at the Special Olympics games when she runs a race or throws a ball. She has a whole cheerleading squad in our family. And when she decides to write a book, I see that it gets published.

So here is a much-edited version of Jezreel's first book. We have just moved again from Tennessee to Colorado Springs, and from what I can tell, this book is about a big party. It takes place in a castle, with all her friends, old and new. Enjoy!

"Team Castle" by Jezreel Allen

There's going to be a party! My name is Jezreel and I Love Parties! This Party will be in a big green Castle. I am the party planner and I have been busy mak cards for all my guest My favorite saying, besides "Best Day ever!" is "Teamwor makes the dreamwor

I have so many friends old and new and we are all on different team. My first team is my family! we will be working together on this party to make it the best party ever! Dad will be working with Biggest Brother on forts and Tree house behind the castle. Biggest sister with be greeting all the guests and ~~help~~ help mom with tons of food! We will have all my favorites: lasagne, spaghetti and fried rice with all kinds of cake, pie and cookies for dessert. other Brothers will be helping with the ~~mais~~ and ~~takeing~~ out the

Trash and blowing up TONS of balloons, my sisters wiss be pleading art activites, reading books and arranging flowers. Iss going to be supper fun! Working on teams is fun becacse we all guet to help and we all get to do what we are good aff.

My friends old and new, and teachers to are invited to this party. We are all on different teams and I have given each team a no name. Sometime silly names! Like "Team spy!!" team anfil and Team silly White Rice! Team work makes the dream work! even barney, Dora and barbie are coming to this event! In the evening, we will have a big slumber party in all the upstairs bedroom at the castle. we will watch lots of videos and eat breakfast burritos. When we wake up. all my friends, old and new

Be there. As guests
arrive, they will see
flowers on each side
of the front castle
gate. We will all be so
happy to finally be all
together! We
will have all kinds of
games inside and out
side. And balloons
of every color. There
will be a big barn out
Back for all the
animals. It will be so
amazing because we'll
actually be able to
play at the park, and
at the beach, all at
This one castle.

Did I mention all
of the food?! And
all the hot chocolate,
hot chocolate tea,
and Hot Apple cider
we want; my mom
will be very besy
with all this food as
she is Chief food
maker but my
family will help he
There will be rainbo
s and balloons Ever,
where with all the
flowers. This will
truly be the
Best Day

Jezreel's book, "Team Castle," written in her own hand

The Webb Family
Kevin, Sarah, Zeke (age 7), Nate (age 4), Caedmon (age13)

PART TWO: PRAYER MANUAL FOR FINDING ORPHANS A FOREVER HOME

Sarah and Kevin Webb

10

Prayers for the Children and Families

GOD, WE PRAISE YOU BECAUSE we know You are for the orphan. We know Your plan is to use us to father the fatherless. You have made this clear in Your Word by stating, "Pure and undefiled religion before God and the Father is this: to visit orphans and widows in their trouble, and to keep oneself unspotted from the world" (James 1:27, NKJV).

God, You love these children more than we ever could. You saw purpose and plan for each one of their lives before they were created in their mother's womb. Forgive us for not consistently and boldly obeying Your commands. Give us Your heart for these children. Do not let us become overwhelmed by the large numbers of orphans, but rather help us see the children as You see them, created uniquely with purpose and value. Develop within us a longing to know their names and hold them in our arms.

God, we ask that You send Your angels to guard the orphans. Place a barrier of protection around them as they wait on their families. Protect their minds, bodies, and spirits from any attack from the Enemy. Place caregivers in their lives who love them, love You, and that will lead them to You while they wait on their families.

God, I pray that Your people will sense a strong calling on their lives to adopt and foster children. We pray for a spirit of adoption to be released on Your church. Holy Spirit, arrest hearts and raise up moms and dads who fiercely love You and are willing to chase after these children. Help those who are called to adopt or foster step into this calling boldly. Do not let the barriers that we see in our flesh discourage us from Your calling to go. Launch us today, God, and place a support system around each and every family that You send.

As You are calling families, open the eyes of the church to see that she is also called to be a support system for these families. Let us see the need to support them as they walk through this process. Call us to stand as support as Aaron and Hur did with Moses (Exodus 17:12). Let us uphold these families as they contend with the Enemy for the lives of the children that You have placed with them. Lord, we all play a part in orphan care, and no part is any more important than the other. Open our eyes to see the need for financial, emotional, and prayerful support. Give us the courage to draw close and love these children as our own. Unite each of us in our callings for this purpose and make it clear what part we are to play in the area of orphan care. Our hearts' desire is to serve You. We say yes to whatever Your call is on our lives. God, blow our minds with what You have in store for each of us. Help us walk boldly and without fear. Use us mightily for Your purposes, God. We trust You!

Passages to Pray

Exodus 17:12

Psalm 68:5–6

Isaiah 43:1

Jeremiah 1:5

Jeremiah 29:11

Matthew 18:10

Matthew 19:14

1 Corinthians 12:14–27

James 1:27

11

Prayers to Be Mobilized

FATHER GOD, THANK YOU FOR being our Abba Father. Thank You for hearing the voices of Your children when we cry out to You. Thank You for the mystery of prayer and for allowing us to partner with You through prayer in accomplishing Your will on earth as it is in heaven. Forgive us when we don't make prayer a priority in our lives. God, cause us to long for consistency rather than complacency in our prayer closets. Lord, John Wesley said that "You do nothing except in answer to believing prayer," and Your Word bears out that concept. And as You have commanded us to pray for laborers for the harvest, we now want to ask You to raise up prayer warriors to stand in the gap for the world's orphans. Motivate the church to call out for the plight of the fatherless. God, burden the hearts of

Your people to cry out for them just as we cry out for our biological children. Call us to spiritually stand in the gap for the lives of these precious children. Bring us together in groups of two or three and groups of hundreds or thousands to intercede for their needs. Teach us to pray for their immediate needs of safety and shelter and sustenance but also for their spiritual needs as well. Remind us to ask You to make their hearts fertile ground, ready to receive the seed of Your love and Your Word. Keep us praying that You would place people in their lives now, wherever they are, to begin leading them to You.

Lord, please raise up families to take orphans in and continue Your work in their lives by being their forever families. Lord, raise up an army, a body of believers that fights through prayer the principalities and powers of this world, the very plans of the Enemy. Overwhelm Your people with the message that while not everyone is called and equipped to take an orphan into their home, we are all commanded to pray continually. Let Your church organize with the specific purpose of praying for orphans, both in general and for very specific children. And then, Lord, let them see firsthand, in very specific and supernatural ways, the fruits of their prayers. Let them see lives changed and Your kingdom advanced because of the prayers of the saints.

Passages to Pray

1 Samuel 12:23

Ezekiel 22:30

Matthew 6:10

Matthew 18:20

Mark 4:8

Luke 10:2

Romans 8:15

Ephesians 6:12

1 Thessalonians 5:16

12

Prayers for God to Jezreel the Seed for Families

FATHER, IN YOUR WORD YOU have given us numerous examples of sowing and reaping, planting and harvesting. And, Lord, there are many different applications of this principle, but we believe one of the strongest and most clear is the principle of raising children in Your kingdom. The Hebrew word *Jezreel* means "to sow." So now, Lord, we pray that You will *jezreel* the seed for families for the fatherless. We pray for the children You have called us to nurture, the fatherless of the nations. We ask You to keep them protected until the time children will be planted in the good soil of a forever family.

We ask You to raise up families with the right set of characteristics so they will have the nutrients needed for the seeds to flourish. We pray, Lord, that potential parents will look beyond what they might see as difficult circumstances and instead be able to see the harvest that they will be a part of if they don't grow weary or give up. Remind them that if they go out weeping, bearing the seed for sowing, they will come back home with shouts of joy, bringing the sheaves with them. Father, we ask You to send the early and late rains on both the seeds and the soils, the orphans and their families. They will both need encouragement, strength, and resources at just the right time. Adoption is not always an easy road, but please remind them that You are the One who gives growth, the One responsible for the very life that we are called to nurture, and that You will bring a harvest of precious fruit as we patiently labor beside You.

Passages to Pray

Deuteronomy 11:14

2 Chronicles 15:7

Psalm 126:6

Psalm 146:9

Proverbs 22:6

1 Corinthians 3:7

2 Corinthians 9:6–8

Galatians 5:22

Galatians 6:9

13

Prayers to Open the Arms of the Church

FATHER, THANK YOU FOR THE body of believers that You have knit together to be Your church. Thank You that there seems to be a shift beginning to take place in the way Your church views its call to care for orphans and widows. We ask for Your forgiveness that our response to that duty has been lax in the past and even now still falls short of the need. We pray, Lord, that You will make Your church see that she is being called for such a time as this. We pray that You will burden the hearts of pastors, leaders, and teachers for the physical and spiritual lives of orphans. We pray that You give them specific genders, faces, and even names of children who desperately need a home. We ask You for strategies and tools to meet the need.

We ask You to raise up people within the church to lead adoption ministries and keep the spotlight shined on orphan care. We ask You to not let us easily forget that when we see one of the least of these in need, that we are really seeing You in need. We come against the plans of the Enemy to distract and blind us with fear or apathy. And we know Father, that when You call us as the church to stand in the gap and meet the needs, that You will also supply the resources that will be required to meet those needs. We ask for Your favor and we praise You for the results that we are confident we will see when we step up to serve orphans.

Caedmon and Zeke

Passages to Pray

Esther 4:14

Amos 3:7

Matthew 6:24–34

Matthew 19:14

Matthew 25:34–40

John 14:15–18

Romans 12:11

Philippians 4:19

2 Timothy 1:7

14

Prayers for Radical Faith

FATHER, YOUR WORD GIVES US numerous examples of radical faith. Noah built an ark because You told him to, even though no one had ever even seen rain. Abraham moved his family to a distant land without even knowing where he was going and was willing to sacrifice the very son that You gave him by promise, simply so he could follow You. By faith, Moses chose to be ridiculed by the people he knew as family in order to lead Your nation out of Egypt and through the Red Sea onto dry land. Joshua saw the walls of Jericho fall because he had radical faith to follow what surely would have seemed to be a crazy plan. We are amazed by the things these patriarchs of the faith saw You do through them. Yet so often, Lord, we forget that they didn't have the rest of the story in front of them to read before they acted. We forget that they, like us, were surely worried and afraid to step out and do the big things You were asking of them. Please remind us that when You ask us to cross the Jordan, the water will always part when our feet get wet. God, call us to do radical things for You. Call us to step out of the boat and walk on the waves through the wind and the rain. Call us to make sacrifices, to sell possessions, to seek funding, to rely on You to provide when we can't see a way. Call us to love children who are hurting beyond our level of experience or ability to handle. Call us to serve You even when our family and friends think we are crazy. Give us the courage to follow You with radical faith. And then, Lord, let us witness You building our arks of provision, leading us to foreign lands, raising up our sons and daughters, and stepping across the barriers that the Enemy was confident would hinder our surging forward to serve You and build Your kingdom.

Passages to Pray

Joshua 1:9

Joshua 3:13

Matthew 14:29

Matthew 19:21

2 Corinthians 9:7

2 Corinthians 9:8

2 Corinthians 10:4–5

Philippians 4:13

Hebrews 11

15

Prayers for the Church to Adopt Plus-One Vision

F ATHER, YOU HAVE TOLD US that where there is a lack of vision the people perish, but we find joy when we keep Your laws. You make it clear in Your Word how we are to treat children. You tell us to let the children come to You. You tell us that children are as arrows in a quiver, a heritage, and a gift from You. You tell us we are to care for orphans and widows. You tell us that when we do good things for "the least of these," we do it for You. But too often, Lord, we get focused on our own agenda and plan. It's as though we're wearing horses' blinders that allow us to focus only on our goals right in front of us and block out the suffering and need around us. Father, remove our blinders and let us see with the eyes of our heart.

Let us see the endless number of orphans in our world as well as their individual faces. Allow us to even hear their individual names. May we see our own sons and daughters in those precious faces. Keep us from sacrificing the meeting of those needs on our altar of having a nicer home or heftier retirement.

Jesus, give us a vision of that day when crowds of laughing children gathered around You. Oh, how huge Your smile must have been! And then, Lord, let us picture ourselves as Your disciples, trying to prevent those precious little ones from getting to You. Then please show us a picture of bringing children to introduce to You so we may experience that incredible joy. Give us the vision of our place in that plan, whether adopting a child into our family, helping to provide resources and support to those who do, or covering them daily in prayer. We each have a vital role to play, Father, and we praise You for making us all a part of Your story.

Passages to Pray

Psalm 119:18

Psalm 127:3–5

Proverbs 29:18

Isaiah 49:16

Matthew 19:14

Matthew 19:26

Matthew 25:40

Luke 14:23

James 1:27

16

Prayers to Release the Father's Heart and the Spirit of Adoption

LORD GOD, WE UNDERSTAND THAT brokenness and the need for adoption was never a part of Your original plan for families. But what a beautiful picture of redemption and grace adoption is! God, You are so faithful to redeem all the broken pieces in our lives. Forgive us for our sins and our messes, and thank You so much for Your plan, rather than our own, for our lives. As Your Word teaches us in Isaiah 55:9, Your ways are higher than our ways, and Your thoughts are higher than all our thoughts. Thank You for Your faithfulness to us.

Father, burn in our hearts a special place for the orphan. Release this spirit of adoption over Your church. Give us Your heart and help us to be willing to walk through fire for these children. Change our hearts to align with Your heart. Help us to lay our obstructed vision aside and see clearly Your calling on our lives. Move upon our hearts and give us a love that causes us to lay down our lives for the sake of Your children. We bind the Enemy's plan to cause fear and hesitation to move forward in our calling, and we replace his fear and hesitation with Your courage and boldness to walk out Your plan. Help us keep our eyes on what we discern spiritually rather than what we see in the flesh. Do not let the words and actions of others cause doubt about what we are called to do. Let our stories be a testimony of Your goodness and cause others to be moved to action because of Your faithfulness through our obedience. God, our hearts' desire is to serve You with our whole life. Use us in any way that would turn others to You. We believe and trust that You are working all things for our good and for the good of Your kingdom, power, and glory forever.

Passages to Pray

Isaiah 55:8–9

Joel 2:25

Matthew 18:18

John 15:13

Romans 8:28

Romans 10:13–14

1 Corinthians 2:14–16

Ephesians 1:5

James 4:3

Daniel's Legacy

Daniel Bart O'Brien, age twenty-eight, a beloved and adopted son, died of a fatal mix of alcohol and drugs on April 1, 2019. Shortly after his death God inspired his parents to purchase and dedicate a multi-unit house in the city of St. Louis to Mission Gate Prison Ministry. The home is simply to be called "Daniel's House." We are excited to announce that we have found and are under contract to buy a four-family flat in the Bevo Mill area!

In Daniel's memory, men who have accepted Christ, fresh out of prison, will be given a second chance to redeem their lives and overcome a messy past. Like King David, we "praise the Lord, O my soul, and forget not all his benefits. He forgives all my sins and heals all my diseases; he redeems my life from the pit and crowns me with love and compassion." (Psalm 103: 2-4)

In each of the four apartments will be a picture of Daniel with his beloved dog and a little bit of his story. Tattooed on his chest were the words, "Always have Faith," and on his prayer card, the words of Luke 1:37: "For nothing is impossible with God."

RESOURCES

Awaken the Dawn - awakenthedawn.org

Bound4LIFE - bound4life.com

Contend Global Ministries - contendglobal.com

Lifeline Children's Services - lifelinechild.org

Love Without Boundaries - lovewithoutboundaries.com

Empowered to Connect - empoweredtoconnect.org

Submit your prayer answer adoption stories - allenfamilyministries.org

ABOUT THE AUTHORS

Samantha and Steve Allen have six children, and one in heaven. They currently live in Colorado Springs and work with Contend Global Ministries.

Sarah and Kevin Webb have three boys. They currently live in Chattanooga, Tennessee, and lead an adoption ministry called Making Room Ministries.

Made in the USA
Monee, IL
03 June 2020

32424205R00075